RAINHILL in Retrospect

Introduction

Nostalgia, someone once said, is a thing of the past. A clever, witty remark, but nostalgia is rather more than this: it is a thing of the past, present and future.

We all have our memories of yesteryear, often distorted by time, but what will our grandchildren have to remind them how we lived?

Precious little!

Lovely, maybe quaint, old buildings have been demolished or their original uses drastically changed; playing games in streets devoid of traffic is now impossible; home entertainment is controlled by a switch on a box in the corner of the room.

Well, now there is something else, modest though it may be. This volume gives us all something to remember about Rainhill.

The people of Rainhill are the ones really responsible for this book. Without them digging into attics, cupboards and drawers, or revealing the contents of lovingly kept volumes, there would be no Rainhill in Retrospect.

It is to them we dedicate this volume, in gratitude, as a heartfelt tribute to our ancestors who left us so much worth remembering. The choice of pictures must, of necessity, be arbitrary: one person's selection is another person's rejection — but the choice was so wide and varied the task was an impossible one.

So, who knows? It might just be possible that, in the style of a Hollywood film title, Rainhill in Retrospect II could be in production in the not-too-distant future.

November, 1992

CROSS MILL LANE

SPECIAL FEATURES

Monster who murdered wives, children —
Pages 32 and 33

World history made in Rainhill —
Pages 62 and 63

Drawings [except pp 32 & 33]
Copyright Jill Dagnall

Published by Rainhill Railway and Heritage Society, The Library, View Road, Rainhill, Prescot, Merseyside L35 0LE
© Rainhill Railway and Heritage Society 1992
ISBN 0 9520446 0 9

Printed by Welshpool Printing Co (1992) Ltd, (0938) 552260. Fax: (0938) 553614

Rainhill Station in LNWR days (Pre 1923)

Foreword

by Harry Johnson
Chairman, Rainhill Railway & Heritage Society

Why Rainhill in Retrospect? For some time it has been suggested there should be some recorded photographic history of Rainhill, and the real impetus for this came from the public.

It was their reaction to the highly successful photographic exhibition held in the local library in April, 1991, entitled Bygone Rainhill, that led directly to the publication of this book.

The Society, mindful of the tremendous public response to the exhibition looked at ways and means of providing and financing some form of publication.

The result is Rainhill in Retrospect.

The village is rich in history, which has been well researched and magnificently presented in a number of publications at extremely reasonably prices, but the Society felt there was a gap which needed to be filled.

We would like to feel that this book, in which pictures are mainly allowed to tell the village story, will give many happy hours to readers of all ages and generations.

Watchmaking

In the early part of the 19th century Rainhill must have had a fairly flourishing watch business, an offshoot, no doubt, of the world-renowned Prescot industry.

A trade directory of 1825 lists the following:

File cutters: James Bennison, John Critchley, William Molyneux, Henry Plumpton, Thomas Plumpton.

Movement makers: Henry Glover, William Johnson (broach).

Watch tool makers: William Fogg (vice and shears), Thomas Gee (pliers), Robert Nelson, J. Vose (comps), Richard Vose (nipper and fly), John Woods (vice), Thomas Woods (vice).

William Fogg and the two Woods lived at Rainhill Stoops.

Acknowledgments

The production team of Rainhill in Retrospect is grateful to the following major sponsors:

MANWEB plc, Liverpool District, Lister Drive, L13 7HJ.
A1 Fencing, Mill Lane, Bold Heath, Widnes.
Widnes Car Centre, Moor Lane, Widnes.
Rainhill Civic Society.
Rainhill Labour Club.

Many scores of people, not merely from Rainhill, have loaned pictures, and those used are gratefully acknowledged: Miss G. M. Hennin, Mr J. Hopkins, Mr D. Houghton, Mr T. Kay, Mr T. Mangan, Mrs M. J. Oxley, Mr K. Sandywell, Mr A. Tilston, Mr A. Wallace.

Newspaper cuttings reproduced are from the January 31, 1908, issue of the Prescot Recorder and Huyton-with-Roby, Rainhill and District Observer.

A great deal of work involved in the production of this book has been done (voluntarily!) by members of the Rainhill Railway & Heritage Society, Rainhill Civic Society and Rainhill Community Library. Serving in this capacity were Jill Dagnall, Ray Fenton, Wendy Georgeson, Derek Houghton and Ann Slater. Thanks are due to them and also to Mrs V. Hainsworth and staff at the St Helens Local History Library.

Finally, though they would not seek special attention being brought to themselves, the following who have been involved in Rainhill in Retrospect to an even greater extent are worthy of thanks:

Derek Houghton, whose photographic expertise and knowledge of Rainhill history have been vital elements in the selection of pictures;

Chris Tigwell, whose efforts in obtaining sponsorship and the right printers have been incalculable;

Jill Dagnall, whose drawings are proof not only of her great skill but of her love for Rainhill;

Wendy Georgeson, whose dedication to the cause has been unsurpassed, whose willingness to tackle any task however mundane is unrivalled, and whose expertise in getting things done smoothly has made this publication possible.

Finally, those who have been directly involved in the production of this book would like to thank the Committee of the Rainhill Railway and Heritage Society for their support and encouragement and for their confidence that we would produce the goods — on time and to budget!

Readers who would like to delve further into the formal History of Rainhill should refer to "The Story of Rainhill", published by Rainhill Civic Society, and on sale at Rainhill Library.

Typical watchmaker's window, at the rear of a house on Warrington Road.

A bustling, historic scene outside the Victoria Hotel, to mark the start of a daily bus service from Widnes Transporter Bridge to Rainhill in 1914.

4 *A tranquil village scene at the turn of the century. Trees flourished in abundance, traffic was noticeable by its absence. And how those telegraph poles dominated!*

On the high road

A directory of the West Derby Hundred of 1825 describes Rainhill as "being situated on the high road from Manchester to Liverpool, three miles ESE of Prescot: the principal establishment of Mr Bartholomew Bretherton, the great and successful coach proprietor of this place, opposite to his stately mansion."

Also listed in the directory is: "Hanging Birch" — some think this should be Hanging Bridge — "a hamlet in the township of Rainhill, four-and-a-half miles SE of Prescot."

A drawing of the turnpike road from Liverpool to Warrington in the 18th century, lists The Holt as "Copt Holt". Kendrick's Cross is shown as "Kenwright's Cross", and the crossroads near what is now the Pilkington garden centre is called "Wild Mare".

RAINHILL HALL. C.1600.

A familiar sight not too long ago was the coal cart delivering fuel. The picture shows Thomas Holden performing just that task, but this was 1909 and he was delivering the contents of his wagon to the Blue Works in Chapel Lane.

A mole catcher, too

A village directory of Rainhill, circa 1825, lists the following: Hugh Abbott, Ship Inn; John Ackers, road surveyor; Miss Barton, ladies' boarding school; Thomas Bradshaw, coal agent; Bartholomew Bretherton, coach proprietor; John Burn & Co, coal proprietors.

Thomas Dakin, Red Lion; James Fellingham, blacksmith; Richard Forshaw, wheelwright; Anthony Garnett, mole catcher; Samuel Henshaw, coach proprietor; Anthony Keys, schoolmaster; Peter Lawrenson, Rainhill Tavern; William Lomax, stone merchant.

John Giller, musician; James Owen, yeoman; James Page, yeoman; Robert Parr, stone merchant; Samuel Pownall, joiner; Peter Robinson, Rainhill Place; John Seddon, yeoman; James Spencer, gentleman; Thomas Walmesley, gentleman.

ST. BARTHOLOMEWS.
R.C. CHURCH.

Shopping before the First World War

Many shops in the centre of the village have changed in character, in style and in business use. Most, though, are still run as family businesses in the way the two premises pictured here were.

Joseph P. Hennin, family grocer and corn dealer, had his premises where Monaghan's shop is now situated. Rowntree's cocoa, Jacob's cream crackers, Bovril and Golden Stream tea were prominently advertised in his window, while standing proudly at the doorway are Jack Bond and Mr Hennin himself, in this specially posed-for photograph taken in 1913.

On the opposite page is a much busier scene, for this was Christmas soon after the turn of the century. An abundance of fowl can be seen, and a large quantity of fruit and vegetables was available — note the huge bunch of bananas!

This flourishing business is now the Wool Shop.

RED LION INN — RAINHILL STOOPS, WHEELWRIGHT'S SHOP AND SMITHY — ABOUT 1800.

Prescot Reporter.

FRIDAY, JANUARY 31, 1908.

A RAINHILL-ROAD ACCIDENT.

With reference to a paragraph which appeared last week under the above heading, Mr. H. Platt writes to say that the horse which fell was not attached to a cart, but was being led to the shoeing smith's, for the purpose of being "sharpened"; and that the accident was solely due to the slippery state of the road. Mr. Platt wishes to dispel any suggestion that the horse was overladen.

A familiar event in Rainhill in bygone days, the Rose Queen Festival. This picture was taken on June 2, 1928, and was probably in the Ivy Farm Estate area.

St. Bartholomews School.

Royalty came through Rainhill on numerous occasions, en route for Knowsley Hall. This was on July 6, 1909, when King Edward VII was on his way to review the troops and there was, as always, a loyal crowd of locals ready to give a cheer. The building is now the Post Office.

WANTED, a young GENERAL, for small family; references required; good wages to suitable person.—Apply 64, Bickerstaffe-street, St. Helens.
3365   516-518

COOK-GENERAL WANTED; age about 30; personal character; two in family; man for all rough work.—Write Lawton House, Rainhill.
3498   518

WANTED, immediately, at Wire Works, Prescot, several Smart GIRLS; also MEN over 18 as machine hands.—Apply Kemble-street Entrance.
3462   518-519

WANTED, THREE LADS for the Broach and Graver trade; must be willing to be bound apprentices.—Apply J. Pritchard (Foreman), Peter Stubs, Ltd., Rainhill.
3497   519

Packhorse Bridge, Rainhill.

Cobbler Patsy and Black Tommy

The village cobbler, Patsy O'Brien, and his assistant, Black Tommy, outside their premises which have been replaced by the Kwik Save store.

The stones were the gateposts of the premises, which were fronted by a small cobbled forecourt, bounded by a sandstone wall. A small iron railing continued the line of this wall to the corner of the newsagent's shop next door.

On this railing were displayed posters of the prominent news of the day, such as the Relief of Mafeking and the Deeming Murders [for more of which see Pages 32 and 33].

Two similar sandstone posts stand to this day in front of the window of the newsagent's at the corner of Warrington Road and View Road. [See picture in page 22].

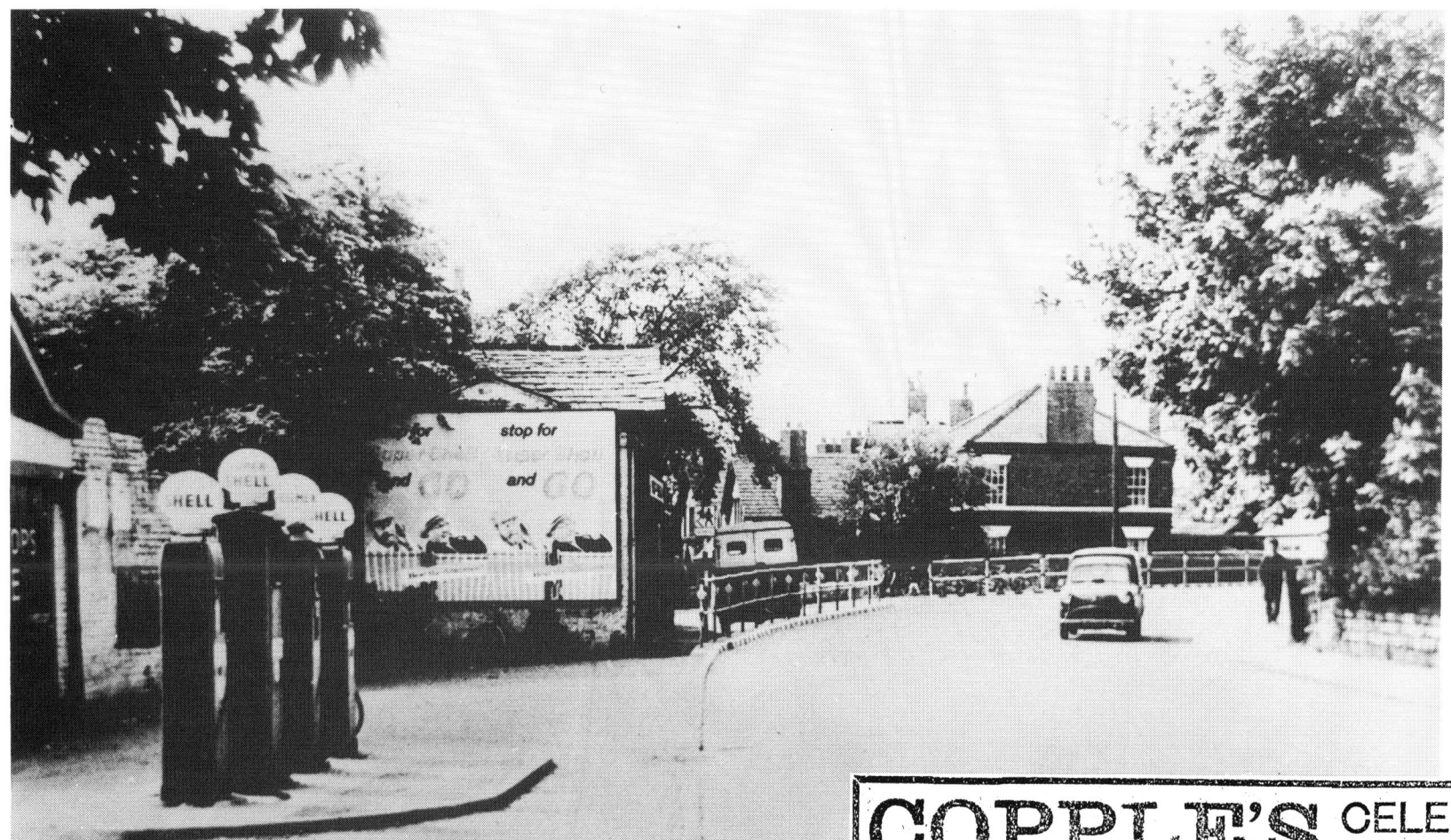

The Stoops bend, little changed today except that the pumps have been re-aligned and the petrol station much modernised.

Happy memories of days when people tended to entertain themselves and others rather than turn a switch. A magnificent band of young men, the Rainhill Morris Dancers of 1931.

A tranquil scene in a truly rural setting. St Ann's Parish Church at its most beautiful, before its crowning glory, the hollow spire, had to be removed as it had become dangerous.

The picture right shows local men working on the removal of the spire after the Second World War.

Below, the newly-built lych gate, through which can be seen the open fields before the houses in Warrington Road were built.

Part of Rainhill that will never be seen again: Cottages leading to the Holt Congregational Church are passed by a tram on its way from Prescot to St Helens. And weren't the poles holding the tram wires ornamental?

Women in the Victorian/Edwardian eras were not quite so helpless as we have been led to believe. At least, this one appears perfectly capable of looking after herself as she takes a whip from a boy in readiness to drive her pony and trap along Old Lane.

The quarry of Welsby and Son in Blundells Lane, parts of which can still be seen, from where came sandstone used in the building of Liverpool Cathedral.

Victoria Street, once the main road from St Helens to Widnes, looking towards Kendricks Cross.

Kendricks Cross in about 1900, from View Road. Note the lamp on the corner of the newsagent's shop, and the iron railings in front of the Victoria Hotel.

St Ann's Schoolchildren, 1907. A rare picture in that almost all the children are named.

Back row: Agnes Howard, Nellie Crompton, Maggie Wilson, Cissie Foster, Elsie Scriven, Gladys Scriven, Winnie Critchley, Annie Cropper, Elsie Critchley.

Second row: May Pentecost, Jennie Jones, Connie Lyon, Edie Holden, Ethel Fitzhugh, Betsy Lee, Elsie Mutch, Alice Booth, Lily Shaw, Lucy Shaw.

Third row: ?? Parr, ?? Saunders, Willie Critchley, Jack Lay, Frank Smith, Edward ??, Jack Parr, Victor Ball, Nellie Lay, Lettie Matthews.

Fourth row: Willie Ball, Margery Smith, Edward Roby, Frank Ormrod, Jack Webb, Fred Davies, John Burchall, Dorothy Ashcroft.

Front row: Willie ??, Jack Welsby, Ernest Hesketh, Herbert Critchley, George ??.

The teacher is believed to be Miss Kerry.

We apologise for errors and omissions.

Royalty or members of the Armed Services were always assured a loyal and hearty welcome from villagers. Here, children from St Ann's school are being mustered to give a cheer for the Yeomanry as they march through Rainhill on their way to fight the Germans in the First World War.

The centre of the village not so long ago. The newsagent's shop is still there, but the Village Snack Bar, Kenwright's shop and the three cottages have gone to make way for Kwik Save. Note the two sandstone pillars alongside the window of the newsagent's, which are referred to in Page 11.

A typical example of a cottage converted into a shop. This was situated in Warrington Road, on the corner of School Lane.

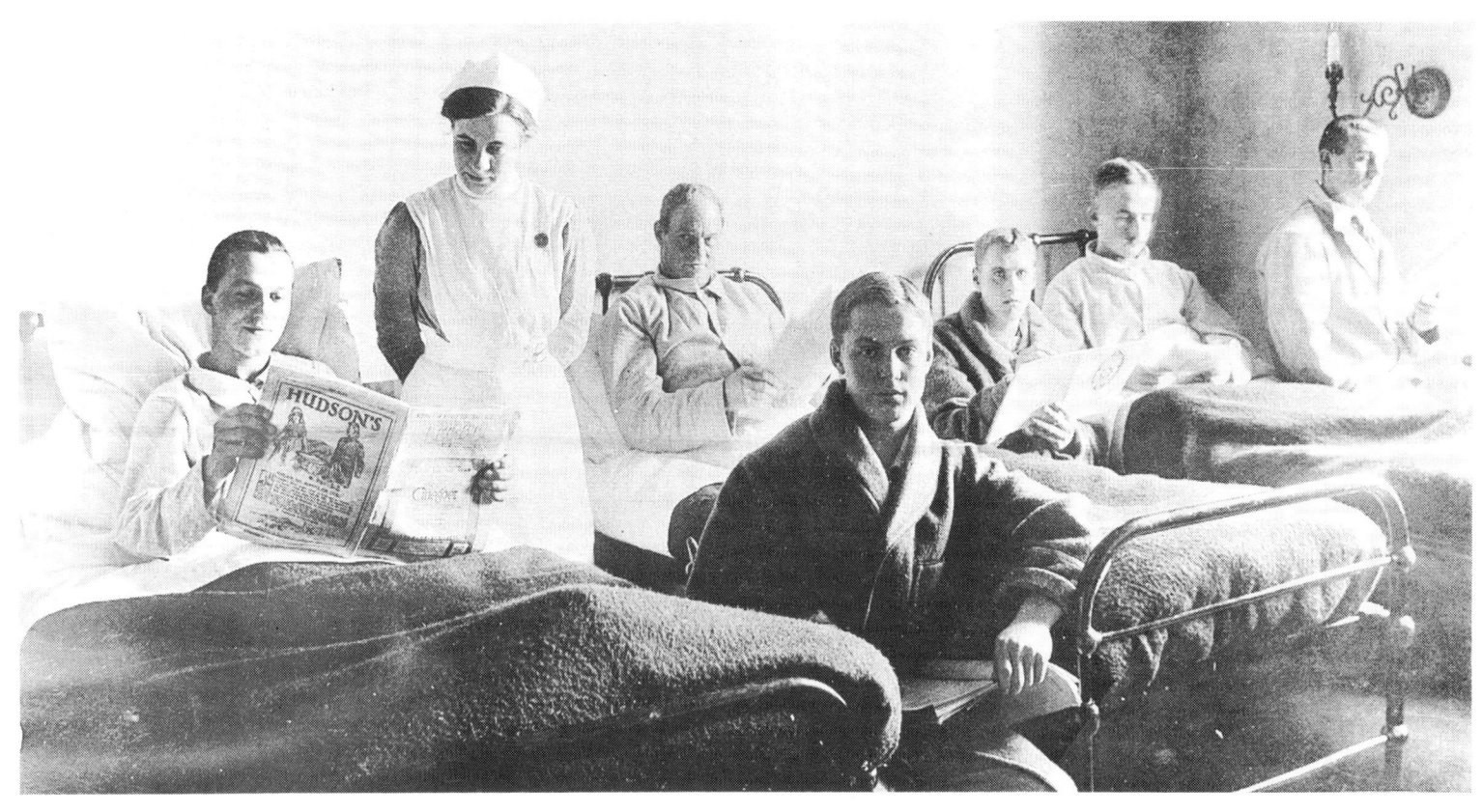

RAINHILL. — CRAVEN LODGE;
semi-detached, three entertaining rooms, six bedrooms, modern conveniences; will be decorated throughout; good garden; five minutes from train and car; rent £40. —Apply The Elms (next door).
3499   518-520

So heavy were the casualties in the First World War that many places were pressed into action to deal with them. The picture above was taken in No 8 Ward at the Tower Hospital, Rainhill, and it is thought the patients were officers. The picture on the facing page was in the form of a greetings card and on it was written: Christmas Wishes, British heroes at Oakdene, Rainhill. This particular Oakdene was at the corner of Owen Road and Lawton Road, where Oakdene Close now is.

The corner of Kendrick's Cross, c 1895, showing one of the new-fangled horseless carriages being much admired.

Roby's Cottages, a fine example of terrace housing of the time, around 1906. They stood in the area that is now Holley Court.

The Hall, Rainhill, pictured in about 1905. The building is now known as Loyola Hall.

An event for which the entire village turned out, from the days when forelocks were tugged. The marriage of Miss Gertrude Stapleton-Bretherton and Commander Dewar, R.N., in 1903. The woman in black is Mrs I. M. Stapleton-Bretherton, daughter of the 12th Lord Petre.

Briar's Hey, Mill Lane, as originally built for John Crossley, chemical manufacturer. It is now a Community Home.

Yet another Royal occasion. Children wait outside the Post Office (now a chip shop) to see the King and Queen as they passed through Rainhill in 1913. Note the water butts outside the Victoria Hotel, and the open-topped bus.

MONSTER WHO MURDERED

Miss Mather's widowed mother

The discovery, in March 1892, of the bodies of a woman and her four children under a layer of concrete in the kitchen of their home, Dinham Villa, Lawton Road, Rainhill, caused a worldwide sensation...and is a topic of conversation in the village to this day.

The story began, so far as local people are concerned, with a happy event: the marriage of Miss Emily Mather, daughter of the local newsagent, to Frederick Bailey Deeming, an officer in the Army, at St Ann's Church.

They left for Australia soon after, and the next news to reach Rainhill was that her body had been found in Melbourne, buried under cement in the kitchen of their home. Australian police contacted Scotland Yard and, as a result of information, detectives made a search of Dinham Villa, home of

WIVES, CHILDREN

Deeming's supposed sister and her four children.

But she was his wife, and when the bodies were dug up it was discovered that she and three of her children had had their throats cut; the fourth child was strangled.

Deeming was tried and hanged in Australia for the murder of Emily Mather: he tried to blame her for the murder of his wife and four children, but nobody believed him especially as the deaths of other "wives" were traced to him.

Several problems were solved by police investigations into Deeming's crimes. Indeed, only one mystery remains.

Dinham Villa was demolished following attacks by ghoulish souvenir hunters: but where is the headstone which marked the grave — three spaces in from the Warrington Road entrance to the churchyard — which once marked the last resting place of a tragic mother and her four innocent children?

Miss Emily Mather

The Rainhill murder victims

In Loving Memory of
MARIE DEEMING, AGED 39 YEARS,
BERTHA DEEMING, AGED 8 YEARS,
MARIE DEEMING, AGED 6½ YEARS,
SYDNEY F. DEEMING, AGED 4 YEARS,
MARTHA DEEMING, AGED 2½ YEARS,
Who were found brutally murdered in Dinham Villa Rainhill, March 16th, 1892,
AND WERE INTERRED IN RAINHILL PARISH CHURCHYARD.

"Nothing in my hand I bring, Simply to Thy Cross I cling."
"These lambs shall not perish."
"Jesus Christ called a little child unto Him."

ST. ANN'S C of E JUNIOR SCHOOL

Sport flourished in Rainhill between the wars as is shown in this picture, c 1930, of the Tennis Club.

An aerial view of Tower College, taken around 1958, showing the sandstone quarry in the background. The smaller picture shows the underpass leading to the quarry, with Mill Lane on the right, and Tower Farm in the background.

A famous place pf recreation in its day, where fishing, especially for carp, was a popular pastime. But The Curling Pond got its name from the fact that the Scottish game of bowls on ice was played there in days when obviously there was more severe weather than we have today. It was situated at the corner of Rainhill Road and Warrington Road: in the background of the picture can be seen Roby's Foundry and the old Commercial Hotel. The pond was filled in in the early 1930's as it had become a danger, especially to children.

The village decorated for the King and Queen to pass c 1914.

Rainhill Old Hall, Blundells Lane, at the turn of the century.

TO LET, "LAUREL MOUNT,"
Prescot-road, three entertaining rooms, four bedrooms, good kitchens, cellars, bathroom (h. and c. water), nice garden back and front; possession January 1st.—Apply J. Lewis, Brooklands, Eccleston, Prescot.
3177   508tfo

Transport systems come and go, and here is a relic, pictured outside the Victoria Hotel about 1900. The name Taylor can be discerned above the shop next to Welsby's butchers.

Trees are still the pride of Warrington Road, but just look how many there were in 1910.

RAINHILL TRADESMEN'S WHIST DRIVE AND DANCE.

Quite 120 persons attended a whist drive and dance in the National Schools, Rainhill, on Monday evening, promoted by the Rainhill Tradesmen. Over 150 persons had expressed their intention of participating in the function, but several of these were kept away by the bad weather which prevailed, but the latter did not interfere with the success of the gathering, which was highly enjoyed. The proceedings opened with the whist drive, and the prizes were won by: 1st, gentlemen, Mr. A. Forshaw; 2nd, Mr. Turner; consolation, Mr. Baldwin. Ladies: 1st, Miss Pickavance; 2nd, Mrs. Cook; consolation, Miss Cookson. Dancing was then engaged in, the music being supplied by Mr. B. Roby, and

Also taken in 1910 was this picture of Old Lane, at the Mill Lane end.

New Road, now called Rainhill Road, looking towards the skew bridge from the Coach and Horses. Note the crossing tram tracks.

Packhorse Bridge - Rainhill.

THE SPYKER CAR.

BARGAINS IN 1907 MODELS
FOR IMMEDIATE DELIVERY.

WRITE FOR PARTICULARS.

British Automobile Commercial Syndicate, Ltd.,
97-98, LONG ACRE, LONDON, W.C.

Chairman: THE RIGHT HON. THE EARL OF SHREWSBURY AND TALBOT
Manager: C. BERTRAND.

3273 510

Following on round the corner from the previous picture is Tasker Terrace, with a tobacconist's shop on the corner. On the left can be seen the street lamp outside the old Coach and Horses, a building which is still standing.

The old Ship Inn, in days when cycling was obviously a popular mode of transport.

> WANTED, a few smart LADS, as apprentices to brass moulding and brass turning respectively.—Apply John Roby, The Brassworks, Rainhill.
> 3504　　　　　　　　　　　　518

A much more up-to-date picture — although it is almost unbelievably 40 years old — of the celebrations in St Ann's School for the Coronation of Queen Elizabeth II.

Pupils of a much earlier era — five-year-olds at Rainhill CE School in the Summer of 1927.

And four years before that, pupils at St Bartholomew's pictured in their school playground.

Church Terrace...with Warrington Road so devoid of traffic these schoolchildren were able to walk down the centre of the carriageway without danger.

TO BE LET, Unfurnished, BROOK COTTAGE, RAINHILL, about half a mile from Lea Green Station, containing two large entertaining rooms, six bedrooms, dressing-room, bathroom, kitchens, etc.; good garden; rent £38; coach house and stable, extra, if required.—Apply to Rawns and Sons, Ltd., Brook Works, Rainhill.
459tfo

WOODBINE VILLAS, Warrington-road, Rainhill. House to Let, containing bathroom, w.c., hot and cold water throughout; rent 8s. 6d. per week, clear.—Apply J. and J. Woods, Reliance Foundry, Rainhill.
3475   518-520

Looking towards Kendrick's Cross from the skew bridge. On the left of T & A Birchall's cab office, can be seen the Bridge Inn. On the right it would appear that a family is flitting: there doesn't seem to have been enough room on the cart for all the household goods as in the foreground a man and woman are carrying items of furniture.

ST. ANN'S

A busy family of butchers preparing for a Royal visit. Note the bull's head on the right-hand door and above the shop near the guttering, and the ram's head just above the woman. And observe the unusual telephone number — 1Y. A pet shop is now on this site.

The corner of Warrington Road and Chapel Lane, showing the magnificent entrance to St Bartholomew's Church. The railing on the left is obviously a convenient resting place for the delivery boy; and, again, note that the sparsity of traffic made it safe for the girls on the right to play with their hoops in the middle of the road.

Miss Ackerley's carriage waits outside the Victoria Hotel, with Miss Margery Fogg looking on.

Fatalities brought footbridge

The opening of the railway created a level crossing where Tasker Terrace and Victoria Street met, and there were a number of accidents with road vehicles at this point, culminating in a fatality on December 3, 1867.

Three horse-drawn carts approached the crossing and the night signalman, William Johnson, opened the gates to allow them through. The first two crossed the lines without mishap but the third, which the signalman tried to turn back, was struck by an express goods train. Mr Johnson and the horse were killed, the cart driver being thrown clear and escaping injury.

At the same time, a wagonette started to cross from the other side. The locomotive struck the horse and shafts throwing the wagonette on to its side. The driver, Thomas Danby, was seriously injured and died the next day. The horse also died.

The passengers, Edward Ackerley, auctioneer, of Longton Villa, and his two sisters, were lucky to escape with bruises.

A petition was sent to the railway company to provide a safer means of crossing, with the result that the present footbridge was erected, and the road from St Helens was continued to Warrington Road, as it is today.

The altar of St Ann's Church decorated for Harvest Festival in 1890. The paintings were covered some thirty odd years ago.

The Stoops, with the Red Lion on the right. The house in the centre is still standing.

View from the skew bridge of Roby's Foundry just before it was demolished.

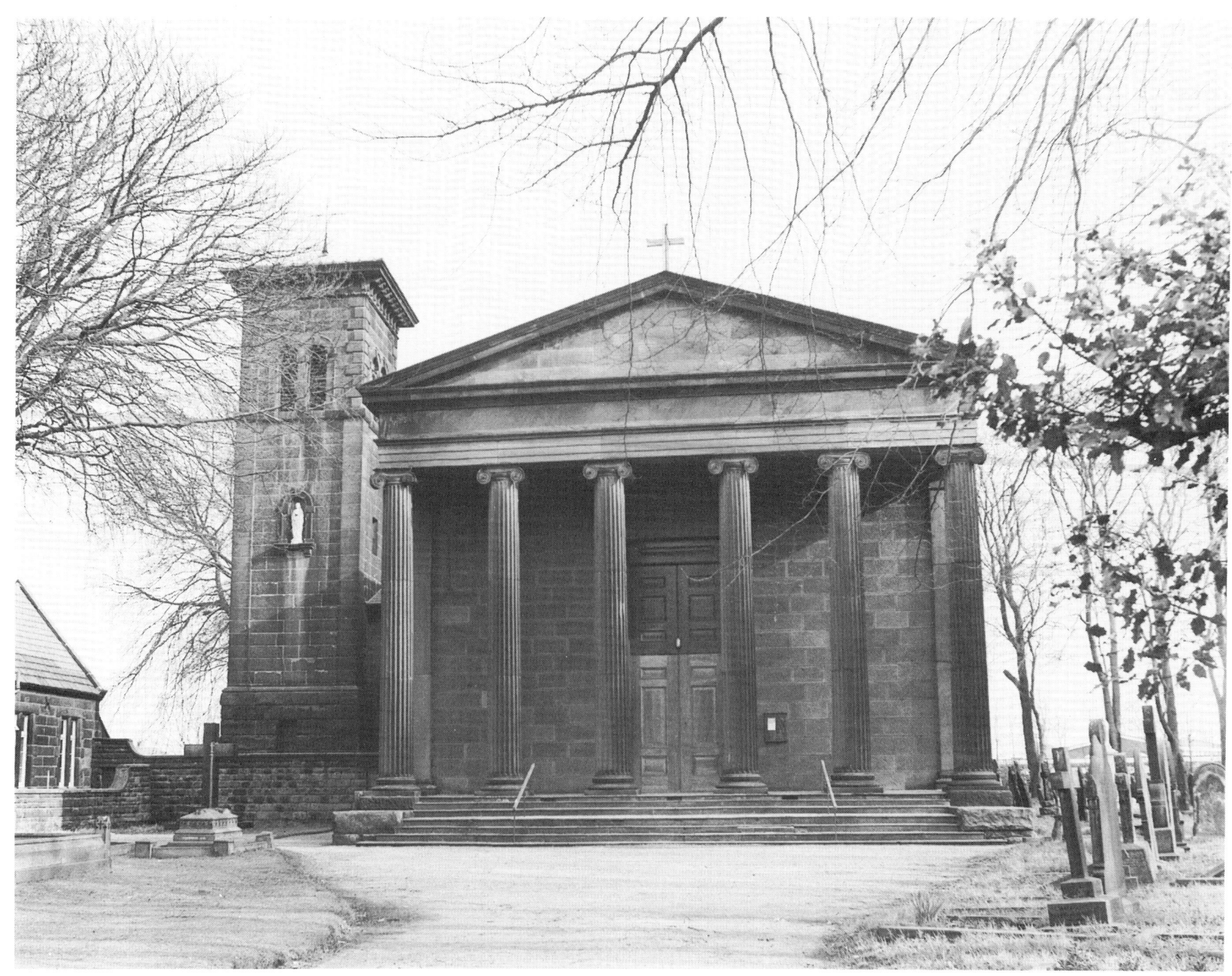

The magnificent entrance to St Bartholomew's RC Church.

Churches

Rainhill is blessed with three fine churches, representing different denominations of the Christian faith. Before the Anglican church — St Ann's — was built in 1839, parishioners had to travel to Prescot, Widnes or Eccleston to attend services.

But within thirty years all three congregations had places of worship of their own.

St Ann's was opened on June 21, 1839, but did not become a separate parish from Prescot until 1869.

St Bartholomew's RC Church was consecrated on August 24, 1840 (the tower was added nine years later), thanks to the generosity of Bartholomew Bretherton [see Page 62].

Finally, the Methodists had their own local place of worship when St James' was certified on June 27, 1860.

Two stages in the development of St Ann's CE Church: Left, the original church of 1838, and right, after the extension and new tower were built in 1843.

St James' Methodist Church in the 1890s, when it was described as the Wesleyan Chapel.

Manor Farm, pictured in the 1960s before it became a public house.

The Post Office (now a chip shop) in 1904, showing the first houses in Houghton Street, with shuttered windows.

Duke's Clough, still a popular walk for villagers, before the M62 was built.

World History

Impression of Rocket passing under Skew Bridge.

If Rainhill was the cradle of a world revolution in transport — the squawking infant steam railway system — the village was also where another global first was conceived, Float Glass, whose birth had to be kept a closely guarded secret for seven years.

The Railway may have been conceived and indeed, born elsewhere, but it was in Rainhill that the weak-kneed toddler was cured of the rickets and given the strength and the will to walk, run and race into history.

The Rainhill Trials is a name known throughout the world, though perhaps few know where the place is, other than that it is somewhere in England. This makes us no less proud of the fact that it was in our village that the trial was held, between October 6 and 14, 1829, on a straight stretch of line less than two miles long, which resulted in the new mode of travel spreading throughout the world.

George Stephenson's Rocket was the winner, and there followed a number of firsts for the area, not least the skew bridge over the line at one end of Rainhill Station, which survives despite the efforts of Dr Beeching to close it.

But for a handful of enthusiasts there would be *nothing* to show of the part Rainhill played in world history. Their efforts in creating a permanent exhibition near the library in View Road cannot be applauded enough. Yet it must be said that the exhibit is to the credit of those local people, members of the Railway & Heritage Society, rather than to the railway industry as a whole.

Sadly there is not enough in the way of a memorial to those momentous events of 163 years ago, but we can still say with pride:

It happened here!

Bartholomew Bretherton, possibly Rainhill's best known inhabitant, owned a coaching service operating from Liverpool to Manchester and London, in 1800. The first stage at which horses were changed was Rainhill, and stables for more than 200 were built next to the Ship Inn.

He invested some of his profits in the village, most notably by establishing a Roman Catholic Church here — St Bartholomew's, named after him and dedicated to the Apostle. The foundation stone was laid in 1838 and the building consecrated in 1840.

An astute businessman, he was among the first to recognise the threat of the railways to his business. When the Liverpool-Manchester line was opened following the Trials, he is said to have placed a bet with

made in Rainhill

a rail enthusiast that he could take a stage coach between the two cities faster than a train could make the journey.

By changing horses much more frequently than was usual he won the bet — and sold his business to the man he had challenged. Then he invested his money in railways.

That, at any rate, is the story handed down from the days of the Rainhill Trials and though it has to be taken with a grain of salt it deserves to be true.

Certainly, if only for the Roman Catholic Church, Bartholomew Bretherton has left a bigger mark on Rainhill village than any one person before or since.

Unlike the railway revolution, the discovery and development of Float Glass has not made an impact on the public imagination. After all, steam engines could be seen, heard and smelled and were dramatically new, while glass has been with us for centuries.

And glass is glass is glass!

Nevertheless, Float was an enormous step forward, resulting in the fact that today 95 per cent of the world's flat glass is produced with this process.

It came about with Alastair Pilkington — **not** a member of the St Helens glass-making family despite his name — washing dishes at the kitchen sink in his home in View Road, Rainhill. And he did not — with a shout of "Eureka" or otherwise — get his idea for Float Glass by observing grease floating on the water in the washing-up bowl as legend claims.

What did happen, as he himself tells it, was that his mind was a blank at the time. "Washing-up," he said, "is such a mundane task that I was able to do it while turning my thoughts to another, extremely vital matter."

And the "other matter" concerning everyone at Pilkington's at the time was the need, in the interest of maintaining a world lead in the industry, of devising a more efficient method of producing blemish-free, smoother glass.

Sir Alastair, as he later became, had these thoughts at the kitchen sink in 1952, but it was not until 1959, at a cost of £7m, that the company succeeded in floating molten glass on molten tin to create the perfect product. The rest, as they say, is history.

Now, Float Glass is produced, under licence, in many parts of the world.

Sadly, there is not much in the way of a memorial to those momentous events of 40 years ago, but we can still say with pride:

It happened here!

The Pilkington home in View Road where Float Glass was conceived.

The industrial heartland of Rainhill. Looking across the railway railings towards Roby's Foundry and Melling's Iron Foundry, with the cone of Rainhill Glassworks in the centre.

This chronology (incomplete as it is) gives some indication of the development of Rainhill village. The information has been gathered from various sources.

1086—Domesday survey
1190—Richard de Eccleston granted to Allan, the clerk, his brother, the village of Raynehull
1220—Eccleston granted Rainhill to Roger of Rainhill
1246—Rainhill Hall built
1292—Half of Rainhill passed to Alan de Windle, then to his daughter, Alice, wife of Peter de Brindle. Their grand-daughter, Joanne Brindle, married William Gerard, who inherited the estate
1335—William Gerard transferred his portion of Rainhill to the Gerards of Kingsley
1377—First mention of St Ellyns Chapel
1540—Greengate Quarry, first in area to be mined for coal
1606—John Ogle, of Preston, selected Surveyor General for Prescot, Whiston and Rainhill
1616—Edward Eccleston sold his Manor and Lordship of Rainhill to Thomas Fisher, Esquire, of London
1619—Fisher sold Eccleston Manor to Hugh Ley
1662—Alexander Chorley built, or rebuilt, Manor House at Rainhill
1678—Quakers established Friends' Meeting House in St Helens
1726—Liverpool-Prescot turnpike road opened
1746—Ritherope Hall, Rainhill, passed to a niece of John Cobham when he died
1754—Tollgate installed at Kendrick's Cross to catch any coal carts that did not pass through the Prescot or Sankey gates
1755—Work began on Sankey Navigation (opened 1757, completed 1762)
1757—Ritherope Hall sold to Bartholomew Bretherton
1782—John Wesley preached in the area
1810—First lighting of streets with oil lmaps
1826—Pilkington's glassworks started
1828—Thomas Moore and Company, glass bottle manufacturers, established a glassworks at Kendrick's Cross
1829—Stephenson's Rocket won locomotive trials at Rainhill. Skew bridge completed
1830—Manchester-Liverpool Railway opened
1836—James Owen gave land for churchyard to St Ann's
1838—Foundation stone laid by Bartholomew Bretherton for first Catholic Church in Rainhill
1840—Melling family built first foundry in Rainhill
James Brierly bought 363 sq yd of land at the corner of Warrington Road and View Road, and gave the land and school that was on it to three trustees
1848—Extra land acquired for building infants' school on to the school in View Road
1849—First Catholic school in Rainhill built in School Lane by Bartholomew Bretherton, at a cost of £350
1851—Rainhill Mental Hospital opened
1857—Congregational Mission opened at The Holt
1860—First Methodist Mission erected in Rainhill, with 11 trustees
1870—Rainhill Gas and Water Company formed
1875—Iron Congregational Chapel built at corner of Warrington Road and Longton Lane
Extra land acquired to build boys' and infants' school in View Road; further extended in 1880
1881—Two moieties of Rainhill united under one owner
First horse tramways operated on St Helens-Prescot route
1889—First steam tram
1890—Emmanuel Church built at The Holt